Sixteen-year-old Ken Ling watched in horror as his classmates beat up their teacher Mr. Chen. The students battered the 60-year-old with fists and broomsticks. Every time Chen passed out, his tormentors splashed water on him to revive him.

"Kill Me!"

The students tortured Chen for six hours.

"Why don't you kill me? Kill me!" Chen pleaded in agony. He collapsed one last time, and the students finally left him to die in the hallway of their school.

Young Versus Old

Chen's murder was just one act in a wave of violence that was sweeping across China. Young people had joined a war against the older generation. Children were turning on their parents, and students on their teachers.

Under Mao's Command

The Cultural Revolution had begun. Its soldiers—young people like Chen's murderers—did not worry about being punished for their brutality. They had been urged on by the most powerful and beloved man in China: Chairman Mao Zedong.

The Question

Why would the leader of a country start something as violent as the Cultural Revolution? What would make a person follow orders to commit violence against innocent people?

PREVIEW PHOTOS

PAGE 1: Red Guards—young people who fought for Mao during the Cultural Revolution—punish prisoners by pulling their arms into the painful "airplane position."

PAGES 2-3: Holding up copies of Mao's Little Red Book, Red Guards march through the streets of Beijing.

PAGES 4-5: Mao Zedong reviews Chinese troops at Tiananmen Square in Beijing in 1967.

Book Design: Red Herring Design/NYC **Photo Credits:** Photographs © 2012: Alamy Images/Sally and Richard Greenhill: 38, 45 top right; AP Images: 28, 34, 44 bottom, 45 bottom; Bridgeman Art Library International Ltd., London/New York/Private Collection/© The Chambers Gallery, London: 26, 35; Corbis Images: 12, 13, 40 (Bettmann), 37 (Wally McNamee), 16 (Hu Nan/Xianhua Press); Getty Images: 41, 45 center right (AFP), 25 (Sarah Ashun), 42 (Go Chai Hin/AFP), 20 (Hulton Archive), 45 center left (Keystone Features), 43, 45 top left (Rolls Press/Popperfoto), 44 center left (Topical Press Agency); Magnum Photos/Henri Cartier-Bresson: 15; Mark Summers: cover; NEWSCOM: 44 top left (ICC/Imaginechina/ZUMA Press), 2, 3 (RIA Nowosti/akg-images), 1, 30 (Zhou Thong/akg-images); ShutterStock, Inc.: 44 center right (Atlaspix), back cover (Michael Drager); Sovfoto/Eastfoto: 19; The Granger Collection, New York: 4, 5, 8, 10 (Rue des Archives), 44 top right (ullstein bild); The Image Works: 18 (Mary Evans Picture Library), 32 (RIA Novosti), 22 (Roger-Viollet).

Maps by XNR Productions, Inc.

Library of Congress Cataloging-in-Publication Data
McCollum, Sean.
The Chairman : Mao unleashes chaos in China / Sean McCollum.
p. cm. — (Xbooks)
Includes bibliographical references and index.
ISBN-13: 978-0-545-32935-4
ISBN-10: 0-545-32935-3
1. Mao, Zedong, 1893-1976—Juvenile literature. 2. Heads of state—China—Biography—Juvenile literature. 3. China—History—1949-1976—Juvenile literature. I. Title.
DS778.M3M37 2012
951.05092—dc23
2011023336

No part of this publication may be reproduced in whole or in part, or stored in a retrieval system, or transmitted in any form or by any means, electronic, mechanical, photocopying, recording, or otherwise, without written permission of the publisher. For information regarding permission, write to Scholastic Inc., 557 Broadway, New York, NY 10012.

Copyright © 2012, 2010 by Scholastic Inc.

All rights reserved. Published by Scholastic Inc. Printed in the U.S.A.

SCHOLASTIC, XBOOKS, and associated logos are trademarks and/or registered trademarks of Scholastic Inc.

Pages printed on 10% PCW recycled paper.

1 2 3 4 5 6 7 8 9 10   40   21 20 19 18 17 16 15 14 13 12

THE CHAIRMAN

Mao Unleashes Chaos in China

SEAN McCOLLUM

CHINESE PEOPLE hold up a portrait of Mao Zedong and copies of his Little Red Book.

TABLE OF CONTENTS

PREVIEW........................1

CHAPTER 1
Leap Forward, Fall Back 10
Mao's revolution runs off course.

The Party Rules 18

CHAPTER 2
A New Revolution 20
With help from a new generation, Mao seeks revenge.

Mao's Little Red Book 25

CHAPTER 3
Rampage!........26
The Red Guards attack.

Map 31

CHAPTER 4
Back from the Brink.........32
With civil war looming, Mao shuts down the Red Guards.

CHAPTER 5
The Lost Generation 38
Mao sends the young troublemakers away.

XFILES...................43

Timeline 44

1

Leap Forward, Fall Back

Mao's revolution runs off course.

It was October 1, 1949. Mao Zedong stood in Tiananmen Square in Beijing, China. Behind him was a two-story-high portrait of himself. As a jubilant crowd chanted "Long live Chairman Mao," he announced the founding of the People's Republic of China. After more than 20 years of civil war, Mao's Communist Party had won control of the country. Mao was now the leader of more than 500 million people.

As chairman of the Party, Mao had his work cut

out for him. More than half of the Chinese people were peasants—farmers who lived in grinding poverty. But Mao promised to transform China from a nation of poor farmers into an industrial powerhouse.

One-Party Rule

Four years later, Mao and the Communist Party launched a Five-Year Plan for the country. The goal was to increase production in factories. In the process, China would become a communist state—a nation in which one all-powerful party controls the economy and everything is shared equally. (In a capitalist system such as the United States, property is privately

owned or owned by corporations.)

The Five-Year Plan turned life in China upside down. Peasants were forced to join huge, Party-run collective farms. The food they produced belonged to the government. The peasants received rations—fixed amounts of food—in return for their labor.

The Party also extended its control over factory workers. Party members organized factory workers into units known as *danweis*. *Danwei* leaders kept detailed files on the workers. Anyone who wanted to change jobs, move, get married, or have children had to get permission from the *danwei*. If anything suspicious appeared in a worker's file, permission could be denied.

MAO LAUNCHED the first Five-Year Plan in 1953. Peasants were forced to leave their private farms to work on huge collective farms.

Personal freedoms shrank under the Five-Year Plan, but the Chinese economy grew. New schools and roads were built. Doctors and teachers went to the countryside to open health clinics and schools. New factories were built and electric power was extended into rural areas.

Great Leap Forward?

Mao's second Five-Year Plan was launched in 1958. This plan was even more ambitious than the first. Bridges, canals, and dams would spring up everywhere, Mao declared. Every town would have its own airplanes. Highways would double as runways. "If capitalism can do it," Mao demanded, "why can't we?"

To meet the new goals, peasants were forced to work even harder. Collective farms were combined into bigger units called communes. Peasants toiled day and night in the fields. Many were forced to build furnaces in their backyards to produce steel. Hundreds of thousands more peasants were relocated to work on irrigation projects or in factories.

Within a year it became clear that the second

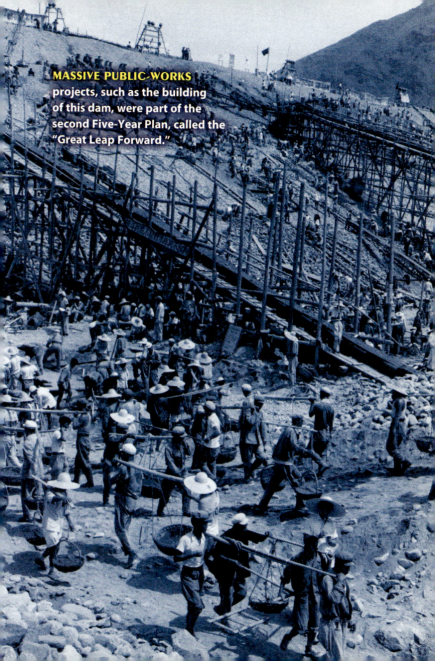

MASSIVE PUBLIC-WORKS projects, such as the building of this dam, were part of the second Five-Year Plan, called the "Great Leap Forward."

A DROUGHT struck China in 1959. Rice crops were destroyed, and millions of people died of starvation.

plan, called the "Great Leap Forward," was failing. Much of the steel produced in the backyard furnaces was unusable. Badly built dams collapsed, and tens of thousands of people drowned.

In 1959 a deadlier catastrophe struck. Drought hit the countryside and turned crops to dust. Peasants starved. Families sold their children to survive; husbands sold their wives. Cannibalism was reported.

Even as his people starved, Mao did not let up. Party members tortured people for hoarding even a morsel of food. One father was forced to bury his son alive because the boy had stolen a handful of grain.

Meanwhile Mao sold huge amounts of food to other countries. It was the only way to pay for the technology he needed to modernize China.

By 1961 between 20 and 30 million Chinese people had starved to death.

Mao seemed unmoved by the suffering. "It is better to let half the people die so that the other half can eat their fill," he said at one Party meeting.

Falling Backward

In the decade since Mao had come to power, few people had challenged his decisions. But with millions dying of starvation, Mao's comrades found the courage to speak up. They insisted on a change of direction.

Mao, now 70, gave up his title of president of China. But he kept the more powerful position of chairman of the Communist Party.

In 1962 Mao's replacement as president, Liu Shaoqi, admitted that the Great Leap Forward had failed. "People do not have enough food, clothes, or other essentials. There is not only no Great Leap Forward, but a great deal of falling backward."

Mao retreated to the background. But he fumed privately that his comrades had challenged him. He began hatching plans for revenge.

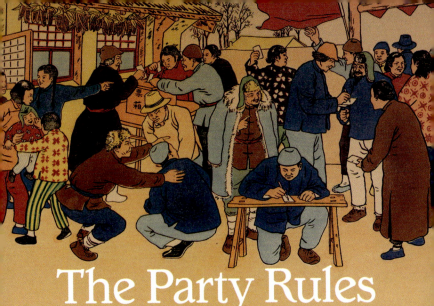

The Party Rules

Here's a snapshot of China's government during the 1960s.

POPULATION XXL
The Communist Party ruled a huge country. There were about 735 million people in China—more than three times the population of the U.S. Most of them were peasants and laborers. They were sometimes referred to as "the masses."

DEMOCRACY? NOT SO MUCH
China's constitution established local, district, provincial, and national groups called congresses. The masses could vote for representatives to their local congresses. Then each local congress elected representatives to the next level.

The catch? These congresses had no real power. Mao and other top members of the Party made all the important decisions. Those decisions were approved without debate by the lower congresses.

FREE SPEECH? NO
Mao cracked down hard on dissent. During his first three years in power, more than a million people were executed

IN DEPTH

THIS PROPAGANDA ILLUSTRATION shows people voting in a Chinese village in 1951.

for opposing communism. According to one person, no one dared to speak up against the government: "Everyone has learned the technique of double talk. What one says is one thing; what one thinks is another."

NEIGHBORS: NOSY
Mao and the Communist Party encouraged the masses to spy on each other. Spies from "Order-Keeping Committees" searched every neighborhood, factory, and collective farm for signs of dissent. Committee members searched people's homes and garbage for letters or books that might suggest anti-communist beliefs. They listened under windows for the sounds of non-communist songs. They pressed friends to inform on friends, children on their parents, and workers on their bosses.

SCALES OF JUSTICE: TILTED
Most trials were carried out by local People's Courts, which had been formed by the Communist Party. The judges on these courts had no legal training. They had been appointed because they'd shown loyalty to communist ideas. The courts often held trials in public to set an example for the masses.

To gain the loyalty of the masses, the courts usually handed down especially harsh sentences for landowners and wealthy businesspeople.

THE CHAIRMAN: MAO
Mao would dominate the Chinese government from 1949 to 1976.

LANDOWNERS wearing dunce caps are marched through a Chinese village in the 1950s.

2

A New Revolution

With help from a new generation, Mao seeks revenge.

In 1964 copies of a slim, pocket-size book began to appear all across China. The book was titled *Quotations from Chairman Mao Zedong*. But it was better known as "The Little Red Book." It included selections from Mao's speeches and writings. At the urging of Mao's defense secretary, Lin Biao, hundreds of millions of copies were printed and distributed.

The Little Red Book was part of Mao's plan to restore his image as China's beloved leader—and strike back at his rivals. In May 1966 Mao and his allies in the Party leadership announced that enemies of the revolution had "sneaked into" the Party. He called them "revisionists" and "counter-revolutionaries." And he claimed that they were plotting to seize power and destroy communism in China.

The Chinese people were told to show their devotion to Mao by exposing suspected enemies of communism wherever they could be found. "Chairman Mao is the

THE CHINESE PEOPLE were taught to idolize Chairman Mao.

red sun in our heart," reported the government-controlled newspaper, the *People's Daily*. "Whoever dares to oppose him shall be hunted down and obliterated." Every day the Chairman's picture appeared on the front page of the paper. Party propaganda offices churned out millions of posters and buttons featuring photos of Mao. Workers, soldiers, and students were required to study The Little Red Book daily.

Destroying the Old

Young people zealously took up Mao's cause. The sons and daughters of Party leaders recruited friends to join political groups. On June 2, 1966, a group of students in Beijing raised a banner in support of Chairman Mao. They called themselves the "Red Guards." More groups of Red Guards quickly sprang up in major cities across China. "We will be brutal!" they warned suspected enemies of communism. "We will strike you to the ground and trample you!"

On August 18, one million young people gathered for a rally in Beijing's Tiananmen Square. Most of them wore green military-style clothes with red strips of cloth tied around their arms—the uniform of the Red Guards.

The crowd roared its approval when Mao arrived at dawn. He, too, wore a simple green army uniform. One of the Red Guard leaders stepped forward to pin a red armband on the Chairman.

Mao could no longer speak clearly, so Lin Biao spoke on his behalf. Lin reminded the Red Guards how they had grown up hearing heroic tales of the revolution. Today, he told them, China would begin a new revolution—*their* revolution.

The students, Lin commanded, must stamp out "The Four Olds": old ideas, old culture, old customs, and old habits. They must destroy all who stood in the way of communism and Chairman Mao: "landlords, rich peasants, counter-revolutionaries, bad elements, and Rightists."

The Cultural Revolution had begun.

IN DEPTH

Mao's Little Red Book

Between 1964 and 1976, more than one billion copies of *Quotations from Chairman Mao Zedong* were published. Mao and his allies wanted this collection of his writings distributed throughout China, and hundreds of printing presses were built to make that happen. Here are a few selections from the "The Little Red Book."

Mao's writings were required reading in China.

"**Unity** of the masses, the Party, and the whole country is essential."

"It is the responsibility of all to **cultivate** themselves, and study Marxism-Leninism [communist theory] deeply."

"**Revolutions** and revolutionary wars are inevitable in class society, and without them it is impossible . . . for the people to win political power."

"The Communist Party does not fear criticism because . . . the **truth** is on our side, and the basic masses, the peasants and the workers, are on our side."

3

Rampage!
The Red Guards attack.

"Don't be afraid of chaos," Mao told the Red Guards. "The more chaos and disorder, the better."

The Chairman made it easy for young people to follow his instructions. Schools and universities closed so students could devote themselves to the new revolution. Red Guards were given free train passes to travel the country and spread the revolution's message.

Mao's allies in the Party leadership urged the new revolutionaries to attack anyone suspected of betraying the communist cause. Red Guards beat up classmates whose grandparents had fought against the Communists during the civil war. They stopped people on the street with Western-style haircuts and shaved their heads. Anyone who enjoyed European music or books came under suspicion. Teenagers accused their friends and parents. Coworkers and neighbors were terrorized into turning each other in.

School officials became special targets of Red Guard thugs. "On the athletic field, every few days, several teachers would be taken out and shot in public," remembered one instructor.

TWO MEN ACCUSED of being counter-revolutionaries are forced to wear signs around their necks and driven through the streets of Beijing by the Red Guards.

Chinese writers and artists were also brutalized. Lao She, a 67-year-old author, was one of the first victims. He was taken to a former temple with other well-known artists and scholars. Their heads were half-shaved in what were called "yin-yang haircuts." Then their tormentors forced them to kneel, poured black ink over their heads, and beat them. When Lao finally made it home, his clothes were so crusted with blood they had to be sliced off. The next day he drowned himself.

Local police were warned not to interfere with the Red Guards. "My view is that if people are killed, they are killed; it's no business of ours," said Mao's security minister. "If the masses hate bad people so much that we cannot stop them, then let us not insist."

Bonfire of "The Olds"

The cultural riches from China's 4,000 years of history also came under attack. In city after city, libraries, museums, and homes were ransacked. Ancient sculptures were dragged into the street and smashed with sledgehammers. Furniture, books, paintings, musical instruments, and priceless antiques were thrown into piles and set on fire. One bonfire in the city of Amoy burned for three days and nights.

In just weeks, thousands of years of irreplaceable treasures were reduced to dust and ash. It was all part of Mao's campaign to erase the past and create "a blank sheet of paper" on which he could write China's future.

IN DEPTH

Mao's China

Mao Zedong ruled Communist China from 1949 to 1976.

KEY

A Mao was born in 1893.

B In 1959 and 1960, famine caused partly by Mao's economic policies killed a quarter of the population in parts of central China.

C Mao launched the Cultural Revolution in 1966, turning millions of young Red Guards loose to destroy "old ideas, old culture, old customs, and old habits."

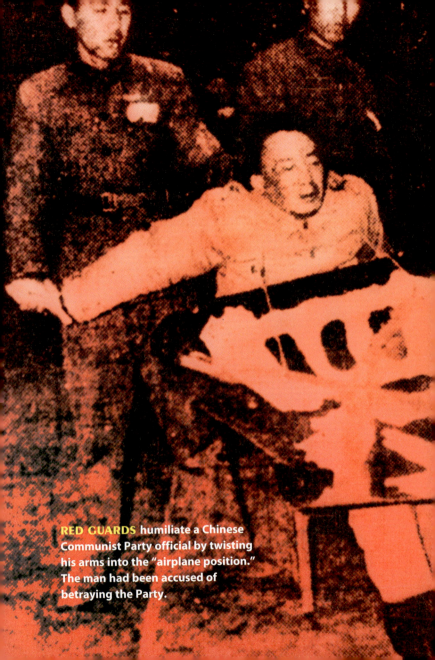

RED GUARDS humiliate a Chinese Communist Party official by twisting his arms into the "airplane position." The man had been accused of betraying the Party.

4

Back from the Brink

With civil war looming, Mao shuts down the Red Guards.

As the Cultural Revolution gained momentum, Mao's rivals in the Communist Party were singled out for punishment. Many top Party officials were accused of revisionism—straying from the "true" communist path. They were handed over to the Red Guards for punishment.

The young revolutionaries humiliated their victims by subjecting them to "struggle sessions." The largest

THE PANCHEN LAMA, the second most important teacher of Tibetan Buddhism, is subjected to a struggle session in 1964. China has controlled Tibet on and off for hundreds of years.

of these public trials took place in sports arenas before jeering crowds. Victims were forced onto a stage and twisted into the "airplane position." They were pushed to their knees, and their arms were yanked back to resemble airplane wings. Signs listing their supposed crimes dangled from their necks. Pinned into this position, the accused endured beatings that sometimes lasted for hours.

Some victims were executed afterward; others killed themselves. Survivors lost their jobs. Many were shipped off to the countryside for "re-education" and to do hard labor on farms.

Mao made sure that President Liu Shaoqi fell victim

to the violence. In 1962 Liu had overturned most of the policies of the Great Leap Forward. Now he would pay for opposing Mao. He begged to be allowed to retire quietly to the countryside. But Mao left him to the Red Guards. Liu and his wife were publicly beaten. They were jailed. Their children were shipped to the countryside to work on farms. Liu eventually died from pneumonia after his guards refused to allow him to receive medical care.

A PROPAGANDA POSTER proclaims, "Down with Liu Shaoqi!"

About-face

By the summer of 1967, China was on the brink of another civil war. Red Guards had overthrown Party leaders in several provinces. Some Red Guard units had begun looting China's military bases to arm themselves. They fought with workers' groups for control over local governments. Finally even Mao had to admit that his revolution was spinning out of control.

After more than a year of bloody chaos, Mao turned against the Red Guards. He publicly accused them of "suspecting everyone and overthrowing everyone." In July 1968 he ordered all Red Guard units to disband.

Only one power remained that could restore order to the country: the People's Liberation Army (PLA) and its five million soldiers. PLA forces were sent into the provinces to reopen schools. Army officers took control of local governments. Where necessary, troops used force to disarm the Red Guards. By the end of 1968, the army controlled most of China's local governments.

The most violent period of the Cultural Revolution was coming to a close. Mao, now 75, had to figure out how to rebuild his terrorized country.

PEOPLE'S LIBERATION ARMY soldiers stand in formation in 1972.

IN A PROGRAM called the "Down to the Countryside Movement," Mao sent former Red Guards and other urban youths to rural areas to "toughen up."

5

The Lost Generation

Mao sends the young troublemakers away.

Two years of violence had left China in chaos. Schools had been closed while millions of young people took part in the Cultural Revolution. Industrial production had fallen drastically. Fewer jobs were available, and crowds of unemployed young people wandered city streets. Mao worried that former Red Guards would continue to cause trouble when they returned to their schools and neighborhoods.

In late 1968 Mao decided on a solution: "The intellectual youth must go to the country and be educated by living in rural poverty," he announced. The policy became known as the "Down to the Countryside Movement."

In the next two years, five million urban youths were sent to rural villages to work beside peasant farmers. These young Chinese were known as "rusticated youth." They included former Red Guards, Red Guard victims, and recent high school graduates.

Life After Mao

After several years of failing health, Mao died on September 9, 1976. One month later, four Party members—including Mao's wife, Jiang Qing—were

MAO DIED in 1976. His body was preserved and put on display in Tiananmen Square in Beijing.

arrested. Called "The Gang of Four," they were found guilty of the worst abuses of the Cultural Revolution and imprisoned. They received much of the blame for what Mao had set in motion.

The Cultural Revolution was officially over. But it had destroyed much of China's rich history and many of its brightest minds. Altogether it left about one million people dead. Millions more young people had been sent away to rural areas. Most of them missed the chance to go to college and be trained as professionals. They are sometimes referred to as China's "lost generation."

JIANG QING at her trial. She was convicted of being a counter-revolutionary and sentenced to life in prison.

Few Chinese people who lived through these events are willing to talk about their experiences. Former Red Guards are ashamed of the destruction they caused. Many of their victims do not want to remember the pain and humiliation they suffered.

A HUGE PORTRAIT of Mao still hangs in Tiananmen Square.

But some Chinese don't want the world to forget. The writer Dai Qing is one of them. A relative of hers was buried alive by the Red Guards. On the fortieth anniversary of the Cultural Revolution, she told a reporter from BBC News, "Only when we can tell all the stories of that time, without censorship, only then will we know what happened and why it happened."

Mao's portrait still hangs in Tiananmen Square. And the Chinese government continues to honor Mao as the country's founding father, although the Party admits that his policies were only partly successful. Yes, he united China and ended three decades of civil war. But those accomplishments came at an appalling cost. ✖

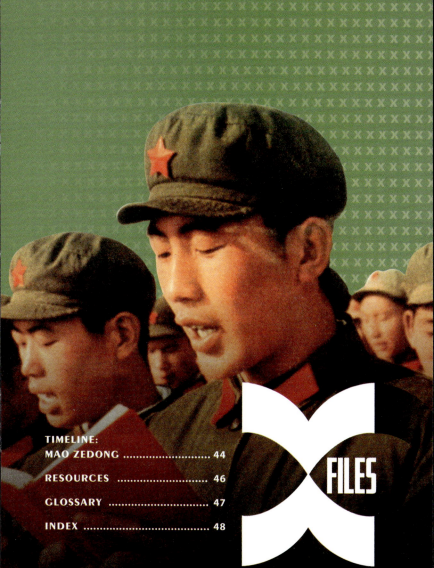

TIMELINE:
MAO ZEDONG 44

RESOURCES 46

GLOSSARY 47

INDEX 48

Timeline: Mao Zedong

DECEMBER 26, 1893: Mao Zedong is born in Hunan province, China.

1934: The Nationalists drive the Communists out of their stronghold in Jiangxi province. Mao leads his army on a desperate retreat known as the "Long March."

1893 1927 1934 1949 1953

1949: Communists win the civil war and form the People's Republic of China.

1953: Mao launches the first Five-Year Plan to industrialize China.

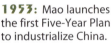

1927: Civil war begins between the Nationalist Party and the Chinese Communist Party.

IN DEPTH

1957: In the "Hundred Flowers" campaign, Mao asks for an honest debate on the future of China. Then he cracks down on anyone who criticizes the government.

1964: Lin Biao publishes *Quotations from Chairman Mao Zedong*—known as The Little Red Book—and vows to distribute it to 99 percent of the Chinese population.

1968: Mao uses the army to put down Red Guard revolutionaries. He sends former Red Guards to work on farms in the "Down to the Countryside Movement."

| 1957 | 1959-1961 | 1964 | 1966 | 1968 | 1976 |

1959-1961: A famine caused by Mao's Great Leap Forward kills more than 25 million people.

1976: Mao dies at age 82. The Gang of Four—including Mao's wife, Jiang Qing (pictured)—are blamed for the Cultural Revolution and imprisoned.

1966: The Cultural Revolution begins with a huge rally in Beijing.

RESOURCES

Here's a selection of books and websites with information about Mao Zedong and the Cultural Revolution in China.

What to Read Next

NONFICTION

Gay, Kathlyn. *Mao Zedong's China.* Minneapolis: Twenty-First Century Books, 2008.

Geyer, Flora. *Mao Zedong: The Rebel Who Led a Revolution.* Washington, DC: National Geographic, 2007.

Heuston, Kimberley Burton. *Mao Zedong* (A Wicked History). New York: Franklin Watts, 2010.

Jiang, Ji Li. *Red Scarf Girl: A Memoir of the Cultural Revolution.* New York: HarperCollins, 1997.

Li-Marcus, Moying. *Snow Falling in Spring: Coming of Age in China During the Cultural Revolution.* New York: Farrar, Straus and Giroux, 2008.

Malaspina, Ann. *The Chinese Revolution and Mao Zedong in World History.* Berkeley Heights, NJ: Enslow Publishers, 2004.

Shane, C.J., ed. *Mao Zedong* (People Who Made History). New York: Greenhaven Press, 2004.

FICTION

Compestine, Ying Chang. *Revolution Is Not a Dinner Party.* New York: Henry Holt, 2007.

Yue, Guo, and Clare Farrow. *Little Leap Forward: A Boy in Beijing.* Cambridge, MA: Barefoot Books, 2008.

Websites

China's Communist Revolution: A Glossary
http://news.bbc.co.uk/hi/english/static/special_report/1999/09/99/china_50/nodhtml.htm

Learn more about the people and events of the Cultural Revolution at this BBC site.

Heaven on Earth
www.pbs.org/heavenonearth/index.html

This is the online companion to the PBS series *Heaven on Earth, the Rise and Fall of Socialism.* It includes a profile of Mao Zedong and an interview with renowned scholar Merle Goldman about the evolution of communism in China.

GLOSSARY

CAPITALISM (KAP-uh-tuh-liz-uhm) *noun* an economic system in which most property and income belongs to private individuals or corporations

CENSORSHIP (SEN-sur-ship) *noun* the suppression or alteration of printed material, public speech, or other expression that the government considers to be harmful

CHAOS (KAY-oss) *noun* total confusion

COMMUNISM (KOM-yuh-niz-uhm) *noun* a political system in which all property belongs to the government or community and resources are shared by all

COUNTER-REVOLUTIONARY (KOUN-tur-rev-uh-LOO-shuhn-air-ee) *noun* a person who is accused of wanting to undo a revolution, such as the communist revolution in China

DEMOCRATICALLY (dem-uh-KRAT-ik-lee) *adverb* decided on by a popular vote

DISSENT (di-SENT) *noun* political opposition to government policies

DROUGHT (DROUT) *noun* a long spell of very dry weather

ECONOMY (i-KON-uh-mee) *noun* the wealth and resources of a country and the goods and services that are produced

FAMINE (FAM-uhn) *noun* a serious lack of food

NATIONALIST PARTY (NASH-uh-nuh-list PAR-tee) *noun* in China, the political party that overthrew China's monarchy with the goal of creating a modern republic; the Nationalists ruled China from 1928 to 1949

PROPAGANDA (prop-uh-GAN-duh) *noun* biased information that is spread to influence the way people think

REVISIONIST (ri-VIHZ-uh-nist) *noun* a person accused of wanting to alter communism's original, pure principles

REVOLUTION (rev-uh-LOO-shuhn) *noun* an uprising by the people of a country to change the country's system of government

RUSTICATED (RUS-tih-KAY-ted) *adjective* describing those who have learned how to live in the countryside

ZEALOUSLY (ZELL-uhss-lee) *adverb* very enthusiastically

INDEX

Amoy, China, 30

Beijing, China, 11, 23, *28*, 45, *45*
bonfires, 29–30, *30*

capitalism, 12–13, 14
civil war, 11, 28, 35, 42, 44, *44*
collective farms, *12–13*, 13, 14, 19
communes, 14
Communist Party, 11, 12, 13, 16, 17, 18, 19, 22, 24, 25, 27, 28, *32*, 33, 35, 40, 42, 44
congresses, 18
"counter-revolutionaries," 22–23, 24, 27–28, *28*, 40–41, *41*, 45, *45*
Cultural Revolution, 24, 33, 36, 39, 41, 42, 45, *45*

Dai Qing, 42
danweis (worker units), 13
deaths, 16, *16*, 17, 18–19, 28, 29, 34, 35, 40, *40*, 41, 42, 45
"Down to the Countryside Movement," 38, 40, 45, *45*
drought, 16, *16*

executions, 18–19, 28, 34

famine, 16–17, *16*, 45, *45*
farming, 12, *12–13*, 13, 14, 16, *16*, 19, 34, 35, 40, 45, *45*
Five-Year Plans, 12, *12–13*, 13–14, *15*, 16, 44, *44*
"Four Olds," 24, 29–30, *30*

"Gang of Four," 41, *41*, 45, *45*
"Great Leap Forward," 14, *15*, 16–17, 35, 45, *45*

haircuts, 28, 29
"Hundred Flowers Campaign," 45

industry, 12, 13, 14, 16, 19, 39, 44

Jiang Qing, 40–41, *41*, 45, *45*

landowners, 19, *19*, 24
Lao She, 29
Lin Biao, 21, 24, 45

"Little Red Book," *20*, 21–22, 23, 25, *25*, 45, *45*
Liu Shaoqi, 17, 34–35
"Long March," *31*, 44, *44*

Mao Zedong, *10*, 11–12, 14, 16, 17, 18, 19, 21, 22–23, *22*, 24, 25, 27, 30, 33, 34, 35–36, 39–40, *40*, 41, 42, *42*, 44, *44*, 45
map, *31*

Nationalist Party, 44

"Order-Keeping Committees," 19

Panchen Lama (Buddhist teacher), 34
peasants, 12, 13, *12–13*, 14, 16, 18, 19, 23, 24, 25, 40
People's Courts, 19
People's Daily newspaper, 23
People's Liberation Army (PLA), 36, *37*
population, 18
propaganda, 23, *26*, 35
property damage, 29–30, *30*
public-works projects, 14, *15*, 16

"Red Guards," 23–24, 27–28, *28*, 29, *32*, 33, 35, 36, *38*, 39–40, 41, 42, 45
"revisionists," 22, 33
"rusticated youth," 40

schools, 14, 27, 28, 36, 39
spies, 19
steel production, 14, 16
"struggle sessions," *32*, 33–34, *34*

Tiananmen Square, 11, 23, *40*, 42, *42*
Tibet, *34*
timeline, 44–45
torture, 16, *32*, 33–34, *34*

writers, 29, 42

METRIC CONVERSIONS

Feet to meters: 1 ft is about 0.3 m
Miles to kilometers: 1 mi is about 1.6 km